Air Fryer Lunch And Dinner Recipes

50+ Easy Mouthwatering recipes to Master your Air Fryer Like a Pro.

| *Beginner's Guide* |

|May 2021 Edition|

© Copyright 2021 by Alan Ross

Table Of Contents

INTRODUCTION 1
    What is an AirFryer? 2
    What is AirFrying? 3
    Ten Tips to use AirFryer 4
    Cleaning Your AirFryer 5
    Ten Mistakes that You Should Avoid Using an AirFryer 6
        Not having enough air 6
        1.   Too much oil 6
        2.   Avoiding using oil 7
        3.   Forget to preheat 7
        4.   Meat is too wet 7
        5.   The food is pretty small 7
        6.   Wouldn't clean the AirFryer 8
        7.   Not checking the temperature of the food 8
        8.   Too much food to eat 9
        9.   Letting a fatty diet go 9
    Functions of AirFryer 9
    Basic Parts, Accessories, and Their Importance 10
    Benefits of Using an AirFryer 11
    AirFryer Cooking Guide 13

Frequently Asked Questions 13
    Air Frying 13
    Cooking Times 14
    Bakeware 14

LUNCH & DINNER RECIPES 15
    1. Sweet Onions & Potatoes 15
    2. Monkey Salad 15

3 'i Love Bacon' 17

4. Parsley Turkey Stew 18

5. Eggplant Lasagna 18

6. Taco Stuffed Peppers 19

7. Potatoes And Calamari Stew 21

8. Pork And Eggs Bowls 22

9. Eggplant Sandwich 23

10. Almond Chicken Curry 24

11. Pesto Stuffed Bella Mushrooms 25

12. Chickpeas 26

13. Cabbage Stew 27

14. Prosciutto & Potato Salad 27

15. Honey Chicken Thighs 29

16. Chickpea & Avocado Mash 29

17. Lamb Satay 31

18. Masala Meatloaf 31

19. Flank Steak & Avocado Butter 33

20. Italian Lamb Chops 34

21. Mu Shu Lunch Pork 35

22. Sweet Potato Casserole 36

24. Sausage Balls 38

26. Dijon Halibut Steak 40

28. Spiced Salmon And Cilantro Croquettes 42

29. Lime Cod 42

30. Beef Chili 44

31. Sweet Potatoes 45

32. Chicken And Coconut Casserole 46

33. Quinoa And Spinach Pesto Mix 47

34. Quinoa And Spinach Salad 47

35. Steak And Cabbage 49

36. Lamb Stew 50

37. American Hot Dogs 51

38. Mashed Garlic Turnips 52

39. Buffalo Chicken Salad 53
40. Garlic Bacon 54
41. Mozzarella Beef 55
42. Chili Bell Peppers Stew 56
43. Cheese Pies 57
44. Creamy Zucchini Noodle Mix 58
45. Chili Beef Bowl 59
46. Faux Rice 60
47. Mozzarella Burger 61
48. Chicken And Pepper Mix 62
49. Lemon Dill Trout 63
50. Paprika Turkey Mix 64

© **Copyright 2021 by Alan Ross**

All rights reserved. No part of this guide may be reproduced in any form without permission in writing from the publisher except in the case of brief quotations embodied in critical articles or reviews.

Legal & Disclaimer

The information contained in this book and its contents is not designed to replace or take the place of any form of medical or professional advice; and is not meant to replace the need for independent medical, financial, legal or other professional advice or services, as may be required. The content and information in this book have been provided for educational and entertainment purposes only.

The content and information contained in this book has been compiled from sources deemed reliable, and it is accurate to the best of the Author's knowledge, information and belief. However, the Author cannot guarantee its accuracy and validity and cannot be held liable for any errors and/or omissions. Further, changes are periodically made to this book as and when needed. Where appropriate and/or necessary, you must consult a professional (including but not limited to your doctor, attorney, financial advisor or such other professional advisor) before using any of the suggested remedies, techniques, or information in this book.

Upon using the contents and information contained in this book, you agree to hold harmless the Author from and against any damages, costs, and expenses, including any legal fees potentially resulting from the application of any of the information provided by this book. This disclaimer applies to any loss, damages or injury caused by the use and application, whether directly or indirectly, of any advice or information presented, whether for breach of contract, tort, negligence, personal injury, criminal intent, or under any other cause of action.

You agree to accept all risks of using the information presented inside this book.

You agree that by continuing to read this book, where appropriate and/or necessary, you shall consult a professional (including but not limited to your doctor, attorney, or financial advisor or such other advisor as needed) before using any of the suggested remedies, techniques, or information in this book.

INTRODUCTION

It is as easy to cook with an AirFryer as with a microwave. Everyone can do it, and you'll wish you had turned to this brilliant cooking system earlier after only a few uses. This chapter will introduce you to the frying options and optimize your cooking time and crispness. We will explain how to keep your AirFryer clean and recommend some gadgets to make your air frying experience even easier and more enjoyable. Since this chapter will cover the basics of using your AirFryer, the first move is to read your AirFryer's manual.

All AirFryers are special, and there are lots of different models on the market with the appliance's recent increase in popularity. Learning how to use your particular AirFryer extensively is the secret to success and will familiarize you with issues related to troubleshooting and safety features. Reading over the manual and washing all the parts before first use with soft, soapy water will make you feel ready to unleash your culinary finesse!

What is an AirFryer?

An AirFryer is a modern kitchen gadget that cooks food instead of oil, blowing very hot air. It provides a low-fat: food variant, which will usually be served in a deep fryer. As a result, fatty foods such as French fries, fried chicken, and onion rings are generally prepared with no oil or 80 percent less fat than traditional cooking techniques. The AirFryer provides healthy fried foods and dinners, helping you eliminate the calories that come with consuming fried foods while also giving you the crunchiness, flavor, and consistency you crave.

This household appliance works efficiently and rapidly by rotating extremely hot air (up to 400° F) around a food product put in an enclosed space. The heat turns the food ingredient outwardly crispy and dry, but inside soft and moist. You should use the AirFryer on pretty much anything. You will barbecue, bake, and roast, in addition to frying. The range of cooking choices makes any form of meal easy to prepare at any time of day.

What is AirFrying?

Frying air is becoming more popular as it helps you cook delicious meals easily and uniformly with little oil and energy. Below are just some of the reasons you want to turn to air frying: it removes other cooking equipment. Because of the refrigerator, microwave, deep fryer, and dehydrator, you can use your fryer! You can quickly cook perfect dishes for every meal without sacrificing taste in one small device. It cooks faster than conventional methods of cooking. Air frying operates by moving hot air through the oven. This contributes to fast and even to cook, using a fraction of your oven's energy. Many air freezers can be operated at 400° F maximum temperature. Despite this, you can make almost anything in an oven with an AirFryer. It does not use much or no cooking oil. One of the key selling points of AirFryers is that you can produce perfectly cooked food with little to no cooking oil. While it might be appealing to some because it can mean less fat, you will rejoice after your rant because it means fewer calories, which will count if you lose weight. It's got a fast cleanup. You will certainly dirty your cooker with every cooking process, but a thorough cleaning is an Air with the smaller cooking chamber and a removable basket in your fry.

Ten Tips to use AirFryer

They can sound daunting if you haven't used an AirFryer before. How long does cooking take? Will you vacuum it? It can sound terrible.

So, we have gone ahead and completed ten helpful cooking tips to help you get the most out of your fryer.

1. When adding the food, preheat your AirFryer.
2. Please make sure that your AirFryer basket is greased with oil, so nothing sticks.
2. But don't use aerosol non-stick cooking sprays, as they can damage your AirFryer.
4. When cooking fatty foods (such as chicken thighs or bacon), add water to the AirFryer drawer to prevent smoking.
5. Use the drippings collected in the drawer (like bacon fat!) to make sauces and gravies for the skillet.
6. During cooking, shake the basket a few times to ensure everything is browning evenly.
7. Make sure your AirFryer basket isn't overcrowded.
8. And cook them in a single layer for larger products (like whole chicken cutlets or pork chops), and don't stack them.
9. To render cleaning simpler using foil or parchment paper.
10. Make sure your AirFryer has at least 5 inches of space around it.

Cleaning Your AirFryer

Next, ensure the AirFryer is fully cool and unplugged until it is washed. You'll need to clean the AirFryer pan to:

1. Switch off the foundation AirFryer pan. Fill the saucepan with hot water and soap for a pot. Let the pan sink in for 10 minutes with the frying bucket inside.
2. Then properly clean the container, use a sponge or towel.
3. Lift the bowl from the fryer and clean the walls at the bottom and outside.
4. Wash with a sponge or a brush the AirFryer pan.
5. Let air-dry everything, and return to the base of the AirFryer.

To clean the outside of your AirFryer, quickly rub a moist cloth on the surface. Make sure then that all the components are in the correct place before beginning your next cooking adventure.

Ten Mistakes that You Should Avoid Using an AirFryer

AirFryers are now a popular option for most people, especially those who don't have time to prepare all their meals traditionally or those who try to avoid oil, value convenience, and seek an easy-to-use alternative to stoves or ovens.

Although AirFryers come with many advantages and seem easy to use, you still need to look out for some things. Your cooking outcomes rely not only on how you use it but also on what you put in it. Here are some important considerations to make sure you make the best use of your AirFryer.

Not having enough air

Your AirFryer requires ample air and space to allow it to transfer heat across the food for a crispness "all over." A decent 12.5 centimeters of space should be held on both sides of the AirFryer, and it should also be put on a secure surface to ensure proper frying of the food.

1. Too much oil

How much oil do you bring in the fryer? It would be a tablespoon or two. Going overboard with oil will produce food that is not cooked properly. This is because your AirFryer is already moving very hot air as it bakes around your food. According to recipe writer and blogger Jim Mumford, this isn't a deep fryer that requires you to dump in loads of oil.

2. Avoiding using oil

Also, the performance would be influenced by not using enough gasoline. Using a small amount of oil with a non-stick spray will make your food crisper and more brownish, Mumford says.

3. Forget to preheat

An AirFryer has to be hot and that the moment the lock is shut, it will cook the food properly. If it's too cold, it will endure the final effects. It makes a huge difference to preheat your AirFryer by turning it on for about five minutes before bringing the food in.

4. Meat is too wet

An AirFryer can't expel moisture from your food, Mumford says. He advises bringing in breaded or crunchy foods like chicken nuggets or Brussel sprouts for optimal results because of soft and soaked vegetables.

5. The food is pretty small

Foods that are too low for the basket end up sliding through the slots and into the fryer's heating part. They'll fire quickly and flood your kitchen with gas and smoke. A good measure for the food you put in the fryers of your air is anything greater than a regular French fries. It would help if you even attempted to place a piece of food in the basket and see that it slips out as you shake it. If it does, it can't be fried in the fryer; that's a warning.

6. Wouldn't clean the AirFryer

According to the editor of the food health blog Candess Zona-Mendola, besides being unhygienic and harmful for your stomach, food poisoning is another consequence of not cleaning the AirFryer in between uses.

"To purify your AirFryer after every meal that's cooked in it," Zona-Mendola says. Use a bit of dishwashing liquid in hot water. Let the bucket drain so that you don't have to clean off baked-on food as much as it wants. Your AirFryer will keep fresh and your tummy clean for three minutes of your time, and your kitchen does not stink.

7. Not checking the temperature of the food

As for every other cooking gadget, you can still handle your AirFryer, whether it's a barbecue, microwave, or burner.

"People who believe that when food is air-fried, there is no need to test the internal temperatures are cooking up a catastrophe formula," says Zona-Mendola. "You want to make sure you are following the same sanitary practices as you would with any other cooking method."

8. Too much food to eat

If you overcrowd the basket with food, there won't be many exposed surfaces to cook for the heat to pass through. Since the AirFryer easily heats, do small batches to ensure that all the food is fried for the optimum taste and texture. You'll also be able to eat more meals in one sitting with a bigger AirFryer.

9. Letting a fatty diet go

Putting water under the basket at the bottom of the cavity is vital when cooking fatty food.

Functions of AirFryer

Many AirFryers have buttons to help you cook something from grilling the perfect salmon, roasting a whole chicken, or even baking a chocolate cake. These buttons are connected depending on your particular AirFryer to customize the times and temperatures. All the recipes in this book were produced using manual times and temperatures because of the large range of AirFryers on the market.

Any AirFryer allows you to set these up on your own. Even

so, it's important to learn how and when to use the cooking programs on your AirFryer. Although certain AirFryer recipes ask for the appliance to be preheated, this is simply something of a personal choice. Some people are preheating their AirFryers while only adding a few minutes to cooking, which these recipes do.

Basic Parts, Accessories, and Their Importance

Prepare and place your ingredients in the bowl, and then set your timer. The hot air continues to work, and the timer departs with a ding sound until its function is complete, signaling that the food is ready. You will also check the diet to see how it progresses without messing with the fixed time. Once you pull the pan out, the fryer will pause; heating will resume when you place the pan back.

The AirFryer is a simple appliance involving no setup and complexities because it consists of three main items; basket cooking, pan, and main fryer unit. There's the Cooking Basket where you put the food, and it has a basket handle where you put your hand to stop burns or cuts while the AirFryer is turned on while holding the appliance and fried foods. The basket suits to the pan well. The Pan collects the remains of food and excess oil and fits perfectly into the AirFryer, and then we have the Main Fryer Unit that is made up of many parts. Other handy features include a rack, double grill plate, basket, and food separators, which allow multiple dishes to be prepared at once.

Benefits of Using an AirFryer

Low-Fat Meals: Unquestionably, the AirFryer's most important benefit is its use of hot-air circulation to cook food ingredients from all angles, thus eliminating the need for oil use. This allows people on low-Fat: diets to prepare delightfully healthy meals comfortably.

Nutritious Foods and Environment: AirFryers are designed to operate without oils being fattened and create healthier meals with up to 80% less fat. It makes it possible to lose weight; even while reducing calories and saturated fat, you can still eat the fried dishes. Through using this gadget, it becomes better to make a move to a healthy existence. Your home often gets rid of the scent that comes with deep-fried foods that sometimes linger in the environment long after deep frying for many hours.

Multipurpose Use: The AirFryer allows you to multi-task, as multiple dishes can be prepared at once. It is your all-in-one appliance that can grill, bake, fry, and roast the dishes you love! You don't need multiple apps for separate occupations anymore because it will do other things individual machines can do barbecue beef, sprinkle vegetables, and bake the pastry. It acts as an easy substitute for your deep fryer, stovetop, and microwave.

Extremely Safe: Remember how cautious about putting chicken or any other ingredients into the deep fryer? You want to make sure the skin is not leaking and melting the hot oil because it is still really dry. You wouldn't need to think about brunt skin from spillage of hot oil with your AirFryer. It does all of the fryings and is free. However, use cooking gloves when repositioning the fryer to eliminate fire hazards. Also, keep your AirFryer out of reach of the baby.

Quick Clean-Up: The AirFryer leaves no oil, so no mess. Clean-up time is fun because there are deposits of oils on walls and surfaces to wipe, and no brush scraping or scrubbing. Any need to waste hours ensuring everything is squeaky clean. The parts of the AirFryer are made of non-stick material, which prevents food from sticking to surfaces, making it difficult to clean. Such pieces are cleanable and easy to manage. These are also reusable and suitable for the dishwasher.

Save Valuable Time: People with tight deadlines will take advantage of the AirFryer pace to produce tasty meals. For starters, in under 15 minutes, you can make French fries and bake a cake within 25 minutes. You should also enjoy the crispy chicken tenders or golden fries within minutes. The AirFryer is just right for you because you're constantly on the move, so you'll waste less time in the kitchen. It helps you control your daily life, which is hectic and stressful, making your day more manageable.

AirFryer Cooking Guide

Vegetables

FOOD	TEMP	TIME/MINUTES	FOOD	TEMP	TIME/MINUTES	FOOD	TEMP	TIME/MINUTES
Asparagus	400F/204C	5-7	Potatoes	400F/204C	15	Shishito Peppers	390F/198C	6
Broccoli	300F/148C	10	Green Beans	400F/204C	5	Portabella Mushrooms	350F/180C	12
Brussel Sprouts	400F/204C	8-12	Onions	400F/204C	10	Small Potatoes	400F/204C	15
Carrots (baby)	380F/193C	15	Zucchini	400F/204C	12	Mushrooms	400F/204C	5
Corn on the Cob	380F/193C	8-10	Sweet Potato	390F/198C	35-40	Cauliflower	400F/204C	12
Eggplant	400F/204C	15	Baked Potato	390F/198C	35-40	Peppers	400F/204C	15

Meats

FOOD	TEMP	TIME/MINUTES	FOOD	TEMP	TIME/MINUTES	FOOD	TEMP	TIME/MINUTES
Chicken Breast	350F/175C	18-20	Wings (2lbs)	400F/204C	16-20	Eye of Round Steak	400F/204C	8-12
Whole Chicken	360F/182C	75	Chicken Tenders	400F/204C	10-12	Turkey Breast (3 lbs)	360F/182C	40
Drumsticks	380F/193C	25	Burger (fresh)	350F/176C	8-10	Bacon (regular)	350F/175C	6-8
Thighs	400F/204C	18	Meatballs	380F/193C	15	Porkchops (bone in)	380F/193C	15-18
Brats	350F/175C	5	Meatloaf	370F/187C	30-35	Porkchops (boneless)	400F/204C	12-14
Hotdogs	390F/198C	4-5						

Seafood

FOOD	TEMP	TIME/MINUTES	FOOD	TEMP	TIME/MINUTES
Calamari	380F/193C	4	Salmon	400F/204C	10
Tilapia	400F/204C	10-12	Shrimp	400F/204C	8-10

Frozen Foods

FOOD	TEMP	TIME/MINUTES	FOOD	TEMP	TIME/MINUTES	FOOD	TEMP	TIME/MINUTES
Mozzarella Sticks	390F/193C	5-7	Chicken Tenders	380F/193C	12-14	Chicken Nuggets	400F/204C	10-12
Steak Fries	380F/137C	22-25	Fish Sticks	400F/204C	8	Bagel Bites	360F/182C	5-6
Texas Toast	350F/176C	3-4	Pizza Rolls	390F/198C	6-8	Potato Skins	370F/187C	5-6
Hot Pockets	370F/189C	11-13	Chicken Wings	380F/193C	30	Tater Tots	400F/204C	18-20
Shoestring French Fries	400F/204C	1-11	Corn Dogs	400F/204C	6-8			
Potato Wedges (frozen)	350F/175C	25-30						
Sweet Potato (frozen)	380F/193C	25-30						

Baking

FOOD	TEMP	TIME/MINUTES	FOOD	TEMP	TIME/MINUTES
Muffins	300F/148C	15	Cupcakes	300F/148C	15
Cake	300F/148C	30	Brownies	320F/160C	30

Frequently Asked Questions

Air Frying

We love deep-fried food flavors, just not the calories: or mess. Air frying is a perfect way to prepare food fast, conveniently, and in less time. It heats up easily and circulates hot air internally with all the natural juices to cook food and seal uniformly. AirFryers make for safer, easier, and more convenient frying, baking, grilling, and steaming.

Cooking Times

The actual cooking periods in your AirFryer will depend on various factors: the make and size of your machine, the size of the food you are cooking, the thickness of the cuts, the cooking utensils used, and the temperature of items entering the AirFryer basket. Test the food for "doneness" before removing it from the oven, as you learn how your machine operates. If possible, you can use a thermometer. Always start with less time and adjust gradually. Slightly change the time cooking in an AirFryer while modifying a convention dish by boiling it for 20–30 percent less time.

Bakeware

The test always with instructions from your particular computer before using some bakeware for your computer. You can, however, use metal, glass, and silicone in most models. If you're searching for the best crunchy and fried sound, you'll want to cook your things all over your food in the air fry basket with the hot air to circulate.

LUNCH & DINNER RECIPES

1. Sweet Onions & Potatoes

Servings: 6

Cooking Time: 30 Minutes

Ingredients:

- 2 large sweet potatoes, peeled and cut into chunks
- 2 medium sweet onions, cut into chunks
- 3 tbsp. olive oil
- 1 tsp. dried thyme
- Salt and pepper to taste
- ¼ cup s, sliced and toasted

Directions:

1. Pre-heat the Air Fryer at 425°F.
2. In a bowl, combine all of the ingredients, except for the sliced s.
3. Transfer the vegetables and dressing to a ramekin and cook in the fryer for 20 minutes.
4. When ready to serve, add the s on top.

2. Monkey Salad

Servings: 1

Cooking Time: 10 Minutes

Ingredients:

- 2 tbsp butter
- 1 cup unsweetened coconut flakes
- 1 cup raw, unsalted cashews
- 1 cup raw, unsalted s
- 1 cup 90% dark chocolate shavings

Directions:

1. In a skillet, melt the butter on a medium heat.
2. Add the coconut flakes and sauté until lightly browned for 4 minutes.
3. Add the cashews and s and sauté for 3 minutes. Remove from the heat and sprinkle with dark chocolate shavings.
4. Serve!

3 'i Love Bacon'

Servings: 4

Cooking Time: 90 Minutes

Ingredients:

- 30 slices thick-cut bacon
- 12 oz steak
- 10 oz pork sausage
- 4 oz cheddar cheese, shredded

Directions:

1. Lay out 5 x 6 slices of bacon in a woven pattern and bake at 400°F/200°C for 20 minutes until crisp.
2. Combine the steak, bacon and sausage to form a meaty mixture.
3. Lay out the meat in a rectangle of similar size to the bacon strips. Season with salt/peppe.
4. Place the bacon weave on top of the meat mixture.
5. Place the cheese in the center of the bacon.
6. Roll the meat into a tight roll and refrigerate.
7. Make a 7 x 7 bacon weave and roll the bacon weave over the meat, diagonally.
8. Bake at 400°F/200°C for 60 minutes or 165°F/75°C internally.
9. Let rest for 5 minutes before serving.

4. Parsley Turkey Stew

Servings: 4

Cooking Time: 25 Minutes

Ingredients:

- → 1 turkey breast, skinless, boneless and cubed
- → 1 tablespoon olive oil
- → 1 broccoli head, florets separated
- → 1 cup keto tomato sauce
- → Salt and black pepper to the taste
- → 1 tablespoon parsley, chopped

Directions:

1. In a baking dish that fits your air fryer, mix the turkey with the rest of the ingredients except the parsley, toss, introduce the dish in the fryer, bake at 380 degrees F for 25 minutes, divide into bowls, sprinkle the parsley on top and serve.

5. Eggplant Lasagna

Servings: 6

Cooking Time: 30 Minutes

Ingredients:

- → 2 medium eggplants
- → ½ cup keto tomato sauce
- → 1 cup Cheddar cheese, shredded
- → ½ cup Mozzarella cheese, shredded
- → 1 cup ground pork
- → 1 teaspoon Italian seasonings
- → 1 teaspoon sesame oil

Directions:

Slice the eggplants into the long slices. Then brush the air fryer pan with sesame oil. In the mixing bowl mix up ground pork and Italian seasonings. Then make the layer from the sliced eggplants in the air fryer pan. Top it with a small amount of ground pork and mozzarella cheese. Then sprinkle mozzarella with the tomato sauce Place the second eggplant layer over the sauce and repeat all the steps again. Cover the last layer with remaining eggplant and top with Cheddar cheese. Cover the lasagna with foil and place it in the air fryer. Cook the meal for 20 minutes at 365F. Then remove the foil from the lasagna and cook it for 10 minutes more. Let the cooked lasagna cool for 10 minutes before serving.

6. Taco Stuffed Peppers

Servings: 4

Cooking Time: 30 Minutes

Ingredients:

- 1 lb. ground beef
- 1 tbsp. taco seasoning mix
- 1 can diced tomatoes and green chilis
- 4 green bell peppers
- 1 cup shredded Monterey jack cheese, divided

Directions:

1. Set a skillet over a high heat and cook the ground beef for seven to ten minutes. Make sure it is cooked through and brown all over. Drain the fat.
2. Stir in the taco seasoning mix, as well as the diced tomatoes and green chilis. Allow the mixture to cook for a further three to five minutes.
3. In the meantime, slice the tops off the green peppers and remove the seeds and membranes.
4. When the meat mixture is fully cooked, spoon equal amounts of it into the peppers and top with the Monterey jack cheese. Then place the peppers into your fryer.
5. Cook at 350°F for fifteen minutes.
6. The peppers are ready when they are soft, and the cheese is bubbling and brown. Serve warm and enjoy!

7. Potatoes And Calamari Stew

Servings: 4

Cooking Time: 16 Minutes

Ingredients:

- 10 ounces calamari, cut into strips
- 1 cup red wine
- 1 cup water
- 2 tablespoons olive oil
- 2 teaspoons pepper sauce
- 1 tablespoon hot sauce
- 1 tablespoon sweet paprika
- 1 tablespoon tomato sauce
- Salt and black pepper to taste
- ½ bunch cilantro, chopped
- 2 garlic cloves, minced
- 1 yellow onion, chopped
- 4 potatoes, cut into quarters.

Directions:

1. Place all the ingredients in a pan that fits the air fryer and toss.
2. Put the pan in the fryer and cook at 400 degrees F for 16 minutes.
3. Divide the stew between bowls and serve.

8. Pork And Eggs Bowls

Servings: 4

Cooking Time: 15 Minutes

Ingredients:
- 2 eggs, whisked
- 1 and ½ pounds pork meat, ground
- 2 teaspoons olive oil
- ½ cup keto tomato sauce
- Salt and black pepper to the taste

Directions:

1. Heat up a pan that fits the Air Fryer with the oil over medium-high heat, add the meat and brown for 3-4 minutes. Add the rest of the ingredients, toss, put the pan in the machine and cook at 370 degrees F for 12 minutes. Divide into bowls and serve for lunch with a side salad.

9. Eggplant Sandwich

Servings: 2

Cooking Time: 7 Minutes

Ingredients:

- ✓ 1 large eggplant
- ✓ ½ cup mozzarella, shredded
- ✓ 1 tablespoon fresh basil, chopped
- ✓ 1 teaspoon minced garlic
- ✓ 1 teaspoon salt
- ✓ 1 tablespoon nut oil
- ✓ 1 tomato

Directions:

Slice the tomato on 4 slices. Then slice along the eggplant on 4 slices. Then rub every eggplant slice with salt, minced garlic, and brush with nut oil. Preheat the air fryer to 400F. Put the eggplant slices in one layer and cook for 2 minutes at 400F. Then flip the vegetables on another side and cook for 2 minutes more. Transfer the cooked eggplant slices on the plate. Sprinkle 2 eggplant slices with basil and mozzarella. Then add 2 tomato slices on 2 eggplant slices. Cover the tomato slices with the remaining 2 eggplant slices and put in the air fryer basket. Cook the sandwich for 3 minutes at 400F.

10. Almond Chicken Curry

Servings: 2

Cooking Time: 15 Minutes

Ingredients:

* 10 oz chicken fillet, chopped
* 1 teaspoon ground turmeric
* ½ cup spring onions, diced
* 1 teaspoon salt
* ½ teaspoon curry powder
* ½ teaspoon garlic, diced
* ½ teaspoon ground coriander
* ½ cup of organic almond milk
* 1 teaspoon Truvia
* 1 teaspoon olive oil

Directions:

Put the chicken in the bowl. Add the ground turmeric, salt, curry powder, diced garlic, ground coriander, and almond Truvia. Then add olive oil and mix up the chicken. After this, add almond milk and transfer the chicken in the air fryer pan. Then preheat the air fryer to 375F and place the pan with korma curry inside. Top the chicken with diced onion. Cook the meal for 10 minutes. Stir it after 5 minutes of cooking. If the chicken is not cooked after 10 minutes, cook it for an additional 5 minutes.

11. Pesto Stuffed Bella Mushrooms

Servings: 6

Cooking Time: 25 Minutes

Ingredients:

* 1 cup basil
* ½ cup cashew nuts, soaked overnight
* ½ cup nutritional yeast
* 1 tbsp. lemon juice
* 2 cloves of garlic
* 1 tbsp. olive oil
* Salt to taste
* 1 lb. baby Bella mushroom, stems removed

Directions:

1. Pre-heat the Air Fryer at 400°F.
2. Prepare your pesto. In a food processor, blend together the basil, cashew nuts, nutritional yeast, lemon juice, garlic and olive oil to combine well. Sprinkle on salt as desired.
3. Turn the mushrooms cap-side down and spread the pesto on the underside of each cap.
4. Transfer to the fryer and cook for 15 minutes.

12. Chickpeas

Servings: 4

Cooking Time: 20 Minutes

Ingredients:

* 1 15-oz. can chickpeas, drained but not rinsed
* 2 tbsp. olive oil
* 1 tsp. salt
* 2 tbsp. lemon juice

Directions:

1. Pre-heat the Air Fryer at 400°F.
2. Add all the ingredients together in a bowl and mix. Transfer this mixture to the basket of the fryer.
3. Cook for 15 minutes, ensuring the chickpeas become nice and crispy.

13. Cabbage Stew

Servings: 4

Cooking Time: 20 Minutes

Ingredients:

- 14 ounces tomatoes, chopped
- 1 green cabbage head, shredded
- Salt and black pepper to the taste
- 1 tablespoon sweet paprika
- 4 ounces chicken stock
- 2 tablespoon dill, chopped

Directions:

1. In a pan that fits your air fryer, mix the cabbage with the tomatoes and all the other ingredients except the dill, toss, introduce the pan in the fryer, and cook at 380 degrees F for 20 minutes. Divide into bowls and serve with dill sprinkled on top.

14. Prosciutto & Potato Salad

Servings: 8

Cooking Time: 15 Minutes

Ingredients:

- 4 lb. potatoes, boiled and cubed
- 15 slices prosciutto, diced
- 15 oz. sour cream
- 2 cups shredded cheddar cheese
- 2 tbsp. mayonnaise
- 1 tsp. salt
- 1 tsp. black pepper
- 1 tsp. dried basil

Directions:

1. Pre-heat the Air Fryer to 350°F.
2. Place the potatoes, prosciutto, and cheddar in a baking dish. Put it in the Air Fryer and allow to cook for 7 minutes.
3. In a separate bowl, mix together the sour cream, mayonnaise, salt, pepper, and basil using a whisk.
4. Coat the salad with the dressing and serve.

15. Honey Chicken Thighs

Servings: 4

Cooking Time: 25 Minutes

Ingredients:

- 1½ pounds chicken thighs, skinless and boneless
- Salt and black pepper to taste
- ¾ cup honey
- ½ cup chicken stock
- 2 teaspoons sweet paprika
- ½ teaspoon basil, dried

Directions:

1. In a bowl, make a mixture with all the ingredients except the chicken thighs; whisk well.
2. Add the chicken thighs to this mix and toss until the wings are coated.
3. Put the chicken in your air fryer's basket and cook at 380 degrees F for 25 minutes.
4. Divide between plates, serve, and enjoy.

16. Chickpea & Avocado Mash

Servings: 4

Cooking Time: 30 Minutes

Ingredients:

- 1 medium-sized head of cauliflower, cut into florets
- 1 can chickpeas, drained and rinsed
- 1 tbsp. extra-virgin olive oil
- 2 tbsp. lemon juice
- Salt and pepper to taste
- 4 flatbreads, toasted
- 2 ripe avocados, mashed

Directions:

1. Pre-heat the Air Fryer at 425°F.
2. In a bowl, mix together the chickpeas, cauliflower, lemon juice and olive oil. Sprinkle salt and pepper as desired.
3. Put inside the Air Fryer basket and cook for 25 minutes.
4. Spread on top of the flatbread along with the mashed avocado. Sprinkle on more pepper and salt as desired and enjoy with hot sauce.

17. Lamb Satay

Servings: 2

Cooking Time: 25 Minutes

Ingredients:

* ¼ tsp. cumin
* 1 tsp ginger
* ½ tsp. nutmeg
* Salt and pepper
* 2 boneless lamb steaks
* Olive oil cooking spray

Directions:

1. Combine the cumin, ginger, nutmeg, salt and pepper in a bowl.
2. Cube the lamb steaks and massage the spice mixture into each one.
3. Leave to marinate for ten minutes, then transfer onto metal skewers.
4. Pre-heat the fryer at 400°F.
5. Spritz the skewers with the olive oil cooking spray, then cook them in the fryer for eight minutes.
6. Take care when removing them from the fryer and serve with the low-carb sauce of your choice.

18. Masala Meatloaf

Servings: 4

Cooking Time: 20 Minutes

Ingredients:

* 2 cups ground beef
* 1 large egg, beaten
* 2 spring onions, chopped
* 1 teaspoon garam masala
* ½ teaspoon ground ginger
* 1 teaspoon garlic powder
* ½ teaspoon salt
* ½ teaspoon ground turmeric
* ½ teaspoon cayenne pepper
* 1 teaspoon olive oil
* ¼ teaspoon ground nutmeg

Directions:

1. In the mixing bowl mix up ground beef, egg, onion, garam masala, ground ginger, garlic powder, salt, ground turmeric, cayenne pepper, and ground nutmeg. Stir the mass with the help of the spoon until homogenous. Then brush the round air fryer pan with olive oil and place the ground beef mixture inside. Press the meatloaf gently. Place the pan with meatloaf in the air fryer and cook for 20 minutes at 365F.

19. Flank Steak & Avocado Butter

Servings: 1

Cooking Time: 40 Minutes

Ingredients:

* 1 flank steak
* Salt and pepper
* 2 avocados
* 2 tbsp. butter, melted
* ½ cup chimichurri sauce

Directions:

1. Rub the flank steak with salt and pepper to taste and leave to sit for twenty minutes.
2. Pre-heat the fryer at 400°F and place a rack inside.
3. Halve the avocados and take out the pits. Spoon the flesh into a bowl and mash with a fork. Mix in the melted butter and chimichurri sauce, making sure everything is well combined.
4. Put the steak in the fryer and cook for six minutes. Flip over and allow to cook for another six minutes.
5. Serve the steak with the avocado butter and enjoy!

20. Italian Lamb Chops

Servings: 2

Cooking Time: 20 Minutes

Ingredients:

⇨ 2 lamp chops

⇨ 2 tsp. Italian herbs 2 avocados

⇨ ½ cup mayonnaise 1 tbsp. lemon juice

Directions:

1. Season the lamb chops with the Italian herbs, then set aside for five minutes.
2. Pre-heat the fryer at 400°F and place the rack inside.
3. Put the chops on the rack and allow to cook for twelve minutes.
4. In the meantime, halve the avocados and open to remove the pits. Spoon the flesh into a blender.
5. Add in the mayonnaise and lemon juice and pulse until a smooth consistency is achieved.
6. Take care when removing the chops from the fryer, then plate up and serve with the avocado mayo.

21. Mu Shu Lunch Pork

Servings: 2

Cooking Time: 10 Minutes

Ingredients:

⇨ 4 cups coleslaw mix, with carrots 1 small onion, sliced thin

⇨ 1 lb cooked roast pork, cut into ½" cubes 2 tbsp hoisin sauce

⇨ 2 tbsp soy sauce

Directions:

1. In a large skillet, heat the oil on a high heat.
2. Stir-fry the cabbage and onion for 4 minutes until tender.
3. Add the pork, hoisin and soy sauce.
4. Cook until browned.
5. Enjoy!

22. Sweet Potato Casserole

Servings: 6

Cooking Time: 60 Minutes

Ingredients:

- 3 big sweet potatoes; pricked with a fork
- 1 cup chicken stock
- 1/4 tsp. nutmeg; ground
- 1/3 cup coconut cream
- Salt and black pepper to the taste A pinch of cayenne pepper

Directions:

1. Place sweet potatoes in your air fryer; cook them at 350 °F, for 40 minutes; cool them down, peel, roughly chop and transfer to a pan that fits your air fryer.
2. Add stock, salt, pepper, cayenne and coconut cream; toss, introduce in your air fryer and cook at 360 °F, for 10 minutes more. Divide casserole into bowls and serve.

23. Dill Egg Salad

Servings: 3

Cooking Time: 17 Minutes

Ingredients:

- 1 avocado, peeled, pitted
- 5 eggs
- 1 tablespoon ricotta cheese
- 1 tablespoon heavy cream
- 1 teaspoon mascarpone cheese
- ½ teaspoon minced garlic
- 1 pickled cucumber
- 1 tablespoon fresh dill, chopped

Directions:

Put the eggs in the air fryer basket and cook them for 17 minutes at 250F. Meanwhile, cut the avocado into cubes and put them in the salad bowl. In the shallow bowl whisk together ricotta cheese, mascarpone, and minced garlic. Grate the pickled cucumber and add it in the cheese mixture. Add dill and stir the mixture well. When the eggs are cooked, cool them in the ice water and peel. Cut the eggs into the cubes and add in the avocado. Add cheese mixture and stir the salad well.

24. Sausage Balls

Servings: 6

Cooking Time: 25 Minutes

Ingredients:

- 12 oz Jimmy Dean's Sausage
- 6 oz. shredded cheddar cheese
- 10 cubes cheddar (optional)

Directions:

1. Mix the shredded cheese and sausage.
2. Divide the mixture into 12 equal parts to be stuffed.
3. Add a cube of cheese to the center of the sausage and roll into balls.
4. Fry at 375°F/190°C for 15 minutes until crisp.
5. Serve!

25. Lasagna Spaghetti Squash

Servings: 6

Cooking Time: 90 Minutes

Ingredients:

- 25 slices mozzarella cheese
- 1 large jar (40 oz) Rao's Marinara sauce
- 30 oz whole-milk ricotta cheese
- 2 large spaghetti squash, cooked (44 oz)
- 4 lbs ground beef

Directions:

1. Preheat your fryer to 375°F/190°C.
2. Slice the spaghetti squash and place it face down inside a fryerproof dish. Fill with water until covered.
3. Bake for 45 minutes until skin is soft.
4. Sear the meat until browned.
5. In a large skillet, heat the browned meat and marinara sauce. Set aside when warm.
6. Scrape the flesh off the cooked squash to resemble strands of spaghetti.
7. Layer the lasagna in a large greased pan in alternating layers of spaghetti squash, meat sauce, mozzarella, ricotta. Repeat until all increased have been used.
8. Bake for 30 minutes and serve!

26. Dijon Halibut Steak

Servings: 1

Cooking Time: 20 Minutes

Ingredients:

- 1 6-oz fresh or thawed halibut steak 1 tbsp butter
- 1 tbsp lemon juice
- ½ tbsp Dijon mustard 1 tsp fresh basil

Directions:

1. Heat the butter, basil, lemon juice and mustard in a small saucepan to make a glaze.
2. Brush both sides of the halibut steak with the mixture.
3. Grill the fish for 10 minutes over a medium heat until tender and flakey.

27. Amazing Beef Stew

Servings: 4

Cooking Time: 30 Minutes

Ingredients:

- 2 lbs. beef meat; cut into medium chunks 2 carrots; chopped
- 4 potatoes; chopped 1-quart veggie stock
- 1/2 tsp. smoked paprika
- A handful thyme; chopped
- Salt and black pepper to the taste

Directions:

1. In a dish that fits your air fryer; mix beef with carrots, potatoes, stock, salt, pepper, paprika and thyme; stir, place in air fryer's basket and cook at 375 °F, for 20 minutes. Divide into bowls and serve right away for lunch.

28. Spiced Salmon And Cilantro Croquettes

Servings: 4

Cooking Time: 8 Minutes

Ingredients:

- 1-pound smoked salmon, boneless and flaked 1 egg, beaten
- 1 tablespoon almond flour
- ½ teaspoon ground black pepper
- ¼ teaspoon ground cumin
- ½ teaspoon ground nutmeg
- 1 tablespoon fresh cilantro, chopped 1 teaspoon avocado oil

Directions:

Put the salmon in the bowl and churn it with the help of the fork until you get the smooth mass. Then add an egg, almond flour, ground black pepper, cumin, nutmeg, and cilantro. Stir the ingredients until they are smooth. Preheat the air fryer to 365F. Wet your hands and make the croquettes. Then place them in the air fryer in one layer and sprinkle with avocado oil. Cook the croquettes for 5 minutes. Then flip them on another side and cook for 3 minutes more.

29. Lime Cod

Servings: 2

Cooking Time: 13 Minutes

Ingredients:
- 2 lime slices
- 1 tablespoon lime juice
- 1 teaspoon lime zest, grated
- ¼ teaspoon ground black pepper
- 1 teaspoon sesame oil
- ½ teaspoon chili flakes
- pound cod fillets, boneless

Directions:

Rub the fish with lime zest, ground black pepper, chili flakes, and lime juice. Then brush it with sesame oil. Preheat the air fryer to 400F. Put the cod in the air fryer basket and cook it for 13 minutes. Then cut the cooked fish into halves and top with the sliced lime.

30. Beef Chili

Servings: 4

Cooking Time: 29 Minutes

Ingredients:

- 2 spring onions, chopped
- 2 medium green bell peppers, chopped 1 tablespoon avocado oil
- ½ teaspoon salt
- ½ teaspoon ground black pepper 2 cups ground beef
- 1 teaspoon ground paprika 1 teaspoon chili flakes
- ½ teaspoon white pepper 1 teaspoon ground cumin
- ½ teaspoon ground coriander 1 chili pepper, chopped
- 1 cup beef broth
- 1 tablespoon keto tomato sauce 1 cup lettuce leaves

Directions:

Put the spring onions in the air fryer pan. Add green bell peppers, avocado oil, salt, and ground black pepper. Stir the mixture gently. Preheat the air fryer to 365F and place the pan with vegetables inside. Cook them for 4 minutes. Then stir well. In the mixing bowl mix up ground beef, ground paprika, chili flakes, white pepper, ground cumin, ground coriander, and tomato sauce Put the meat mixture over the vegetables and carefully stir it with the help of the spoon. Add chili pepper and beef broth. Stir the chili gently. Cook it at 365F for 25 minutes. Stir the chili every 5 minutes of cooking. When the chili is cooked, cool it for 5-10 minutes. Then fill the lettuce leaves with chili and transfer in the serving plates.

31. Sweet Potatoes

Servings: 4

Cooking Time: 55 Minutes

Ingredients:

- 2 potatoes, peeled and cubed
- 4 carrots, cut into chunks
- 1 head broccoli, cut into florets
- 4 zucchinis, sliced thickly
- Salt and pepper to taste
- ¼ cup olive oil
- 1 tbsp. dry onion powder

Directions:

1. Pre-heat the Air Fryer to 400°F.
2. In a baking dish small enough to fit inside the fryer, add all the ingredients and combine well.
3. Cook for 45 minutes in the fryer, ensuring the vegetables are soft and the sides have browned before serving.

32. Chicken And Coconut Casserole

Servings: 4

Cooking Time: 35 Minutes

Ingredients:

- 1 lb. chicken breast; skinless, boneless and cut into thin strips
- 4 lime leaves; torn
- 1 cup veggie stock
- 1 lemongrass stalk; chopped
- 1-inch piece; grated
- 8 oz. mushrooms; chopped.
- 4 Thai chilies; chopped.
- 4 tbsp. fish sauce
- 6 oz. coconut milk
- 1/4 cup lime juice
- 1/4 cup cilantro; chopped
- Salt and black pepper to the taste

Directions:

1. Put stock into a pan that fits your air fryer; bring to a simmer over medium heat, add lemongrass, ginger and lime leaves; stir and cook for 10 minutes.
2. Strain soup, return to pan, add chicken, mushrooms, milk, chilies, fish sauce, lime juice, cilantro, salt and pepper; stir, introduce in your air fryer and cook at 360 °F, for 15 minutes. Divide into bowls and serve.

33. Quinoa And Spinach Pesto Mix

Servings: 4

Cooking Time: 15 Minutes

Ingredients:

- 1 cup quinoa, cooked
- 3 tablespoons chicken stock
- ¾ cup jarred spinach pesto 1 green apple, chopped
- ¼ cup celery, chopped
- Salt and black pepper to taste

Directions:

1. Mix all the ingredients in a pan that fits your air fryer; toss.
2. Place the pan in your fryer and cook at 370 degrees F for 15 minutes.
3. Divide into bowls and serve right away.

34. Quinoa And Spinach Salad

Servings: 4

Cooking Time: 15 Minutes

Ingredients:

- 1½ cups quinoa, cooked
- 1 red bell pepper, chopped 3 celery stalks, chopped
- Salt and black pepper to taste 4 cups spinach, torn
- 2 tomatoes, chopped
- ½ cup chicken stock
- ½ cup black olives, pitted and chopped
- ½ cup feta cheese, crumbled
- ⅓ cup basil pesto
- ¼ cup almonds, sliced

Directions:

1. In a pan that fits your air fryer, combine the quinoa, bell peppers, celery, salt, pepper, spinach, tomatoes, chicken stock, olives, and basil pesto.
2. Sprinkle the almonds and the cheese on top, and then place the pan in the air fryer and cook at 380 degrees F for 15 minutes.
3. Divide between plates and serve.

35. Steak And Cabbage

Servings: 4

Cooking Time: 20 Minutes

Ingredients:

- 1/2 lb. sirloin steak; cut into strips
- 2 green onions; chopped.
- 2 garlic cloves; minced
- 2 tsp. cornstarch
- 1 tbsp. peanut oil
- 2 cups green cabbage; chopped
- 1 yellow bell pepper; chopped Salt and black pepper to the taste

Directions:

1. In a bowl; mix cabbage with salt, pepper and peanut oil; toss, transfer to air fryer's basket, cook at 370 °F, for 4 minutes and transfer to a bowl.
2. Add steak strips to your air fryer; also add green onions, bell pepper, garlic, salt and pepper, toss and cook for 5 minutes. Add over cabbage; toss, divide among plates and serve for lunch.

36. Lamb Stew

Servings: 4

Cooking Time: 30 Minutes

Ingredients:

- 1 cup eggplant, cubed
- 2 garlic cloves, minced
- 3 celery ribs, chopped
- ½ cups keto tomato sauce
- 1 pound lamb stew meat, cubed
- 1 tablespoon olive oil
- Salt and black pepper to the taste

Directions:

Heat up a pan that fits the air fryer with the oil over medium-high heat, add the lamb, salt, pepper and the garlic and brown for 5 minutes. Add the rest of the ingredients, toss, introduce the pan in the machine and cook at 370 degrees F for 25 minutes. Divide into bowls and serve for lunch.

37. American Hot Dogs

Servings: 4

Cooking Time: 20 Minutes

Ingredients:

- 3 brazilian sausages, cut into
- 3 equal pieces
- 9 bacon fillets, raw
- Black pepper to taste Salt to taste

Directions:

1. Pre-heat the Air Fryer for 5 minutes at 355°F.
2. Take a slice of bacon and wrap it around each piece of sausage. Sprinkle with some salt and pepper as desired, as well as a half-teaspoon of Italian herbs if you like.
3. Fry the sausages for 15 minutes and serve warm.

38. Mashed Garlic Turnips

Servings: 2

Cooking Time: 10 Minutes

Ingredients:

- 3 cups diced turnip
- 2 cloves garlic, minced
- ¼ cup heavy cream
- 3 tbsp melted butter
- Salt and pepper to season

Directions:

1. Boil the turnips until tender.
2. Drain and mash the turnips.
3. Add the cream, butter, salt, pepper and garlic. Combine well.
4. Serve!

39. Buffalo Chicken Salad

Servings: 1

Cooking Time: 40 Minutes

Ingredients:

- 3 cups salad of your choice
- 1 chicken breast
- 1/2 cup shredded cheese of your choice Buffalo wing sauce of your choice Ranch or blue cheese dressing

Directions:

1. Preheat your fryer to 400°F/200°C.
2. Douse the chicken breast in the buffalo wing sauce and bake for 25 minutes. In the last 5 minutes, throw the cheese on the wings until it melts.
3. When cooked, remove from the fryer and slice into pieces.
4. Place on a bed of lettuce.
5. Pour the salad dressing of your choice on top.
6. Serve!

40. Garlic Bacon

Servings: 4

Cooking Time: 40 Minutes

Ingredients:

* 4 potatoes, peeled and cut into bite-size chunks
* 6 cloves garlic, unpeeled
* strips bacon, chopped
* 1 tbsp. fresh rosemary, finely chopped

Directions:

1. In a large bowl, thoroughly combine the potatoes, garlic, bacon, and rosemary. Place the ingredients in a baking dish.
2. Set your Air Fryer to 350°F and briefly allow to warm.
3. Cook the potatoes for 25-30 minutes until a golden brown color is achieved.

41. Mozzarella Beef

Servings: 6

Cooking Time: 30 Minutes

Ingredients:

- 12 oz. beef brisket
- 2 tsp. Italian herbs
- 2 tsp. butter
- 1 onion, sliced
- 7 oz. mozzarella cheese, sliced

Directions:

1. Pre-heat the fryer at 365°F.
2. Cut up the brisket into four equal slices and season with the Italian herbs.
3. Allow the butter to melt in the fryer. Place the slices of beef inside along with the onion. Put a piece of mozzarella on top of each piece of brisket and cook for twenty- five minutes.
4. Enjoy!

42. Chili Bell Peppers Stew

Servings: 4

Cooking Time: 15 Minutes

Ingredients:

- 2 red bell peppers, cut into wedges
- 2 green bell peppers, cut into wedges
- 2 yellow bell peppers, cut into wedges
- ½ cup keto tomato sauce 1 tablespoon chili powder
- 2 teaspoons cumin, ground
- ¼ teaspoon sweet paprika
- Salt and black pepper to the taste

Directions:

In a pan that fits your air fryer, mix all the ingredients, toss, introduce the pan in the machine and cook at 370 degrees F for 15 minutes. Divide into bowls and serve for lunch.

43. Cheese Pies

Servings: 4

Cooking Time: 4 Minutes

Ingredients:

- 8 wonton wraps
- 1 egg, beaten
- 1 cup cottage cheese
- 1 tablespoon Erythritol
- ½ teaspoon vanilla extract 1 egg white, whisked Cooking spray

Directions:

Mix up cottage cheese and Erythritol. Then add vanilla extract and egg. Stir the mixture well with the help of the fork. After this, put the cottage cheese mixture on the wonton wraps and fold them in the shape of pies. Then brush the pies with whisked egg white. Preheat the air fryer to 375F. Then put the cottage cheese pies in the air fryer and spray them with the cooking spray. Cook the meal for 2 minutes from each side.

44. Creamy Zucchini Noodle Mix

Servings: 2

Cooking Time: 9 Minutes

Ingredients:

- 1 zucchini, trimmed
- 4 oz chicken breast, skinless, boneless
- ¼ cup heavy cream
- 2 oz Parmesan, grated
- ½ teaspoon ground black pepper
- ¼ teaspoon ground paprika
- ½ teaspoon sesame oil
- ½ teaspoon dried basil

Directions:

Make the zoodles from the zucchini with the help of the spiralizer. Then rub the chicken breast with ground black pepper, paprika, and basil. Sprinkle the chicken breast with sesame oil and put it in the air fryer. Cook it for 8 minutes at 400F. Flip the chicken on another side after 4 minutes of cooking. When the chicken is cooked, remove it from the air fryer and place it on the plate. Then put the zucchini zoodles in the air fryer and cook then at 400F for 1 minute. Meanwhile, mix up parmesan and heavy cream and preheat the liquid over the medium heat until the cheese is melted. Then mix up heavy cream sauce and zucchini. Mix it up well. Chop the chicken roughly and top the zoodles with it.

45. Chili Beef Bowl

Servings: 3

Cooking Time: 18 Minutes

Ingredients:

- 9 oz beef sirloin
- 1 chili pepper
- 1 green bell pepper
- ½ teaspoon minced garlic
- ¼ teaspoon ground ginger
- 1 tablespoon apple cider vinegar
- 4 tablespoons water
- ½ teaspoon salt
- 3 spring onions, chopped
- 1 teaspoon avocado oil

Directions:

Cut the beef sirloin into wedges. Then cut bell pepper and chili pepper into wedges. Put bell pepper, chili pepper, and beef sirloin in the bowl. Add minced garlic, ground ginger, apple cider vinegar, water, salt, and spring onions. Marinate the mixture for 15 minutes. Meanwhile, preheat the air fryer to 210F. Put the bell pepper, chili pepper, and onion in the air fryer basket. Sprinkle them with ½ teaspoon of avocado oil and cook them for 8 minutes. Transfer the cooked vegetables in 3 serving bowls. After this, put the beef wedges in the air fryer and sprinkle them with remaining avocado oil. Cook the meat for 10 minutes at 365F. Stir it from time to time to avoid burning. Meanwhile, pour the marinade from the beef and vegetables in the saucepan and bring it to boil. Simmer it for 2-3 minutes. Put the cooked beef in the serving bowls. Sprinkle the meal with hot marinade.

46. Faux Rice

Servings: 8

Cooking Time: 60 Minutes

Ingredients:

- 1 medium-to-large head of cauliflower
- ½ lemon, juiced garlic cloves, minced
- 2 cans mushrooms,
- 8 oz. each
- 1 can water chestnuts,
- 8 oz.
- ¾ cup peas
- ½ cup egg substitute or 1 egg, beaten
- 4 tbsp. soy sauce
- 1 tbsp. peanut oil
- 1 tbsp. sesame oil
- 1 tbsp. ginger, fresh and minced High quality cooking spray

Directions:

1. Mix together the peanut oil, soy sauce, sesame oil, minced ginger, lemon juice, and minced garlic to combine well.
2. Peel and wash the cauliflower head before cutting it into small florets.
3. In a food processor, pulse the florets in small batches to break them down to resemble rice grains.
4. Pour into your Air Fryer basket.
5. Drain the can of water chestnuts and roughly chop them. Pour into the basket.
6. Cook at 350°F for 20 minutes.
7. In the meantime, drain the mushrooms. When the 20 minutes are up, add the mushrooms and the peas to the fryer and continue to cook for another 15 minutes.
8. Lightly spritz a frying pan with cooking spray. Prepare an omelet with the egg substitute or the beaten egg, ensuring it is firm. Lay on a cutting board and slice it up.
9. When the cauliflower is ready, throw in the omelet and cook for an additional 5 minutes. Serve hot.

47. Mozzarella Burger

Servings: 2

Cooking Time: 12 Minutes

Ingredients:

- 4 sausage patties
- 1 teaspoon butter, softened
- ½ teaspoon ground black pepper
- ¼ teaspoon salt
- 1 oz Mozzarella, chopped 4 bacon slices
- Cooking spray

Directions:

Sprinkle the sausage patties with ground black pepper and salt. Then put the cheese and butter on the patties. Make the balls from the sausage patties with the help of the fingertips. After this, roll them in the bacon. Preheat the air fryer to 390F. Put the

bacon bombs in the air fryer and spray them with the cooking spray. Cook the bombs for 12 minutes – for 6 minutes from each side.

48. Chicken And Pepper Mix

Servings: 6

Cooking Time: 20 Minutes

Ingredients:

- 3-pound chicken breast, skinless, boneless 1 tablespoon tikka seasonings
- 1 tomato, roughly chopped
- green bell pepper, roughly chopped 1 tablespoon coconut oil
- spring onions, chopped

Directions:

Chop the chicken breast roughly and put it in the mixing bowl. Add tikka seasonings, bell pepper, and spring onion. Mix up the ingredients and leave for 10 minutes to marinate. Then preheat the air fryer to 360F. Put the chicken mixture and tomatoes in the air fryer basket. Cook the chicken tikkas for 20 minutes.

49. Lemon Dill Trout

Servings: 1

Cooking Time: 10 Minutes

Ingredients:

- 2 lb pan-dressed trout (or other small fish), fresh or frozen
- 1 ½ tsp salt
- ½ cup butter or margarine
- 2 tbsp dill weed
- 3 tbsp lemon juice

Directions:

1. Cut the fish lengthwise and season the with pepper.
2. Prepare a skillet by melting the butter and dill weed.
3. Fry the fish on a high heat, flesh side down, for 2-3 minutes per side.
4. Remove the fish. Add the lemon juice to the butter and dill to create a sauce.
5. Serve the fish with the sauce.

50. Paprika Turkey Mix

Servings: 4

Cooking Time: 20 Minutes

Ingredients:

1 turkey breast, boneless, skinless and cubed

2 teaspoons olive oil

½ teaspoon sweet paprika

Salt and black pepper to the taste 2 cups bok choy, torn and steamed 1 tablespoon balsamic vinegar

Directions:

In a bowl, mix the turkey with the oil, paprika, salt and pepper, toss, transfer them to your Air Fryer's basket and cook at 350 degrees F for 20 minutes. In a salad, mix the turkey with all the other ingredients, toss and serve for lunch.

CPSIA information can be obtained
at www.ICGtesting.com
Printed in the USA
LVHW080143230521
688251LV00002B/111